KNOWING GOD: REFLE[CTIONS]

AND BONUS B[OOK]

GOD'S ABUNDANCE FOR OUR SUFFICIENCY

BY BRIAN JOHNSTON

Published by:

HAYES PRESS CHRISTIAN PUBLISHERS

The Barn, Flaxlands

Royal Wootton Bassett

Swindon, SN4 8DY

United Kingdom

www.hayespress.org

CHAPTER ONE: KNOWING GOD...AN INTRODUCTION

As youngsters they'd attended the same school. One of the two boys had become a Bible preacher. He'd never become famous, but each Sunday he had presented a simple and sincere message from the Bible. His school-friend had gone into an acting career. He'd done very well and had become quite an accomplished performer. He, too, had been raised in a God-fearing home, and although he'd never totally forgotten what he'd learnt in his youth, his career had pushed all thoughts about God well into the background.

When this now famous actor announced his retirement, his friends and admirers provided a celebratory meal for him - to which he, of course, could invite others. The actor remembered his old school-friend, the preacher, and included him in the invitation list. It was an invitation that was accepted, even though the old preacher considered he'd feel more than a little out of place among a company which would include many celebrities from the world of the performing arts.

At the conclusion of the meal, the actor was persuaded to perform for the guests. He agreed with one surprising condition - that his old preacher friend from school-boy days would do the same. He suggested that they both recite the 23rd Psalm. Why he chose the 23rd Psalm no-one knew – perhaps because it was a famous piece of literature or maybe it was because of some of his boyhood memories, some of which could even have been connected with his preacher friend.

The actor went first and his rendition was greeted with tumultuous applause. It was going to be a hard act to follow. But next the somewhat less impressive figure of the preacher stood up and took out his well-used pocket Bible. He read through the Psalm in the same feeling way he'd read it so often before to people on their deathbed. While he read, and even after he'd finished, there was total silence in the room. The actor shook his friend's hand and turning to his guests, he said, "Do you know what the difference is? I know the Psalm; but he knows the Shepherd!" The LORD is my shepherd: so begins Psalm 23. It's my prayer that, God willing, we'll be able to use this psalm as a framework for getting to know God better.

Let's begin by reminding ourselves that in the Bible God shares His personal name with us. That name, as far as we can tell, is 'Yahweh'. I say as far as we can tell because it's not possible to be sure what the original vowels should have been. In the ancient Hebrew it was simply four consonants: YHWH. It was a word, or name, the Jews considered so holy they never spoke it aloud. Whenever they came across it in their public reading of the Old Testament Scriptures they always substituted another word for it. They usually said, "Sovereign Lord" instead of attempting to pronounce the four letters with meaningful vowels.

Then came a time when the Jews began to write all their words with vowels, but they wanted to preserve their custom of reverence for the name of God, so when it came to the YHWH name of God, they inserted the vowels for its spoken substitute: 'Sovereign Lord' (Adonai). This reminded any Jew reading the Old Testament that he must not say the 'Yahweh' name of God, only one of His titles - 'Sovereign Lord'. Some early English Bible students were unaware of this, and they translated the consonants of the one word with the vowels of the other as though it was the hybrid word 'Jehovah'. But, most likely, the name of God we find in the Bible was intended to be pronounced more like "Yahweh".

In many English-language Bibles, this name of God can be identified by the word 'LORD', or sometimes 'GOD', - but written all in capitals. We find the word 'LORD' all capitalized when it occurs in those famous words at the beginning of Psalm 23: the LORD is my shepherd. So this is an example of Yahweh, the name of God.

Let's remind ourselves of the words of this lovely Psalm:

"The Lord is my shepherd; I shall not want.

He makes me to lie down in green pastures;

He leads me besides the still waters.

He restores my soul;

He leads me in the paths of righteousness for His name's sake.

Yea, though I walk through the valley of the shadow of death,

I will fear no evil; for You are with me;

Your rod and y our staff, they comfort me.

You prepare a table before me in the presence of my enemies;

You anoint my head with oil; my cup runs over.

Surely goodness and mercy shall follow me

All the days of my life; and I will dwell in the house of the LORD forever."

(Psalm 23: 1-6)

The Lord reveals himself through His name in seven other ways in the Old Testament. Let's run through them:

- The LORD will provide (Genesis 22:14)

- The LORD your healer (Exodus 15:26)

- The LORD my banner (Exodus 17:15)

- The LORD who sanctifies you (Leviticus 20:8; 21:8)

- The LORD is peace (Judges 6:24)

- The LORD our righteousness (Jeremiah 23:6; 33:16)

- The LORD is there (Ezekiel 48:35)

That's taking them in the order we find them introduced to us in our Bibles, but we'll take them in a different order which I'll explain in a moment. In this book I'd like to share some thoughts with you on each of these statements by means of which God declares His name to us or, we could also say, makes His character known to us. I think it's convenient to attach them to well-known parts of Psalm 23, in that way it might serve as an aide-memoir for us.

After the opening, "the LORD is my shepherd", we have the words, "I shall not want" - to which we can attach the statement: 'the LORD will provide'. With the restful imagery conjured up by words: 'He makes me to lie down in green pastures; he leads me besides the still waters', we can still easily associate the idea of 'the LORD is peace'. 'The LORD your healer' connects with 'He restores my soul'.

'He leads me in the path of righteousness for His name's sake' brings us in thought to 'the LORD our righteousness'. Next comes, 'Yea, though I walk through the valley of the shadow of death, I will fear no evil; for You are with me' - which serves to remind us that 'the LORD is (right) there' with us. The expression, 'the LORD is my banner' is all about celebrating a victory, which we can lay alongside the words, 'You prepare a table before me in the presence of my enemies'. And finally, 'you anoint my head with oil', will remind us of the fact that 'the LORD is the One who sanctifies'- at least it does if we remind ourselves how prophets, priests and kings long ago in Israel were set apart for their sacred service through being anointed with the sanctifying oil of God.

The order of Psalm 23 then is the order we'll follow as we make progress through the remarkable way in which God Himself has revealed His name to us - and in revealing His personal name, of course, He's disclosing the kind of character that's very uniquely His. This is why this book is called 'Knowing God'. It's our prayer that we will get to know and serve God better as a result of studying these marvellous declarations in which God has shown us what He's really like.

CHAPTER TWO: KNOWING GOD...AS PROVIDER

The twenty-third Psalm opens with the words, "The Lord is my shepherd, I shall not want." The world 'LORD' is usually capitalized in our English Bibles to indicate that it's the name of God - sometimes pronounced as Jehovah - but now thought more accurately to be Yahweh. As we've already reminded ourselves, the immediate focus of this Psalm is on a God who provides. The very first book of the Bible shows God to be a provider. Let's take one early example from Genesis chapter 3 (v. 8-21):

> "Then the man [Adam] and his wife [Eve] heard the sound of the LORD God as he was walking in the garden in the cool of the day, and they hid from the LORD God among the trees of the garden. But the LORD God called to the man, "Where are you?" He answered, "I heard you in the garden, and I was afraid because I was naked; so I hid." And he said, "Who told you that you were naked? Have you eaten from the tree from which I commanded you not to eat?"..."Because you ... ate from the tree about which I commanded you, 'You must not eat of it,' "Cursed is the ground because of you; through painful toil you will eat of it all the days of your life. It will produce thorns and thistles for you, and you will eat the plants of the field. By the sweat of your brow you will eat your food until you return to the ground, since from

it you were taken; for dust you are and to dust you will return."

Then we read: "The LORD God made garments of skin for Adam and his wife and clothed them". So we see that, as well as pronouncing sentence, God also provides a covering. He provided clothes of skins for Adam and Eve. It involved the first ever death of a sacrificial animal victim, a sin offering for the offense of the very first man's disobedience. In this way God provided a covering that was more than simply a physical covering of their nakedness. The point is that God Himself was the provider of the first ever sin offering in the history of this world.

Staying in the Bible's first book of Genesis, I want to link in with that, the equally graphic account of God providing another sacrifice. This time it's described as a burnt offering. And it's here we find the first elaboration of the Yahweh name of God. It was when:

> "God tested Abraham. He said to him, "Abraham!" "Here I am", he replied. Then God said, "Take your son, your only son, Isaac, whom you love, and go to the region of Moriah. Sacrifice him there as a burnt offering on one of the mountains I will tell you about." Abraham took the wood for the burnt offering and placed it on his son Isaac, and he himself carried the fire and the knife. As the two of them went on together, Isaac spoke up and said to his father Abraham, "Father?" "Yes, my son?" Abraham replied. "The fire and wood are here," Isaac said, "but where is the lamb for the burnt offering?" Abraham answered,

"God himself will provide the lamb for the burnt offering, my son." And the two of them went on together.

When they reached the place God had told him about, Abraham built an altar there and arranged the wood on it. He bound his son Isaac and laid him on the altar, on top of the wood. Then he reached out his hand and took the knife to slay his son. But the angel of the LORD called out to him from heaven, "Abraham! Abraham!" "Here I am," he replied. "Do not lay a hand on the boy," he said. "Do not do anything to him. Now I know that you fear God, because you have not withheld from me your son, your only son." Abraham looked up and there in a thicket he saw a ram caught by its horns. He went over and took the ram and sacrificed it as a burnt offering instead of his son. So Abraham called that place The LORD Will Provide. And to this day it is said, "On the mountain of the LORD it will be provided" (Genesis 22:1-14).

Abraham had answered his son Isaac based on faith - "God himself will provide the sacrifice for the burnt offering, my son." That faith was fully justified when God did in fact provide a substitute - Isaac. That's why Abraham named the place "Yahweh" or "the LORD will provide". In His providence, God provided a ram which became a burnt offering there in that special place of God's choosing. This first elaboration of the Yahweh name, in which God reveals Himself as the only one who can provide for our needs, is very much in connection with a place.

and he has made that possible. He has done it by actively making "peace through the blood of His cross" (Colossians 1:20). That's the cross of Jesus Christ, God's Son. He's the one that the apostle Paul was describing in his letter to the Church of God at Ephesus when he wrote that Jesus himself "is our peace" (Ephesians 2:14).

In the original language of this great Bible statement, two points are emphasized. First of all, he, and no other, is our peace; and, secondly, he, in his own person, is our peace. Let me try and illustrate the true sense of that for you. I once read a book about missionary work that was carried out among the Sawi people of Netherlands New Guinea – an unforgettable story of primitive jungle treachery in the twentieth century. These people had proved to be very difficult to reach with the Christian message. They were headhunters and cannibals who actually idolised treachery as the supreme value. As you would expect, this posed a tremendous problem for the missionaries (on top of the very real fear of the possibility that they themselves might be eaten!). How could a society bred on hate, and one that thrived on the principle of revenge, possibly be expected to come to understand the self-sacrificing love of God?

The difficulty was intensely practical as well, because every gesture of friendship in such a culture was naturally regarded with suspicion - it really was a matter of life and death to these people. But there was one gesture that was the exception and that was where the missionaries were able to make their breakthrough. It happened suddenly one day, after many years, when they observed how village warfare was avoided in this culture. There was a ceremony – a ceremony which involved the exchange of a "peace-child". The missionaries watched in total amazement as two hostile villages exchanged two children. They had been on the brink of war, but once they had decided on peace, there seems to be only one possible way for them to go about achieving it. It involved great sacrifice for the families who nobly entered into the exchange. With great grief, a family each village gave away its own baby son, and adopted the child from the other village.

This was the only demonstration of friendship that was above suspicion. For if a man could actually give his own son to his enemies, then that man could definitely be trusted! Everyone in the other village who laid their hands on the adopted son was bound by a "covenant of peace" which committed them to not to work violence against the people who had given him. In their way of thinking, it was simply not possible for peace to be brought about without a peace-child. The missionaries at once seized upon this wonderful opportunity to present Jesus to this people as God's "peace-child". It proved to be the turning-point of the experience of the missionaries in trying to reach these people with God's good news.

Remember that, in their culture, the only man that a Sawi tribesman could trust was someone who'd given his son. On the Bible's own testimony, we are called on to trust in the God who has given his own Son, Jesus, for us. As we've already mentioned, the Bible speaks of Jesus as "making peace through his blood, shed on the cross." By nature we are hostile to God, and it took Jesus' death to make it possible for us to have peace with God. When dying on the cross, God's own Son took the blame for all our failures and mistakes whereby we've offended His holiness.

life in God's kingdom on earth was to demonstrate righteousness and peace and joy in the Holy Spirit (Romans 14:17). These verses are no longer talking about the righteousness which is God's gift to us when we believe. No, they're talking about disciples of Christ actually doing the right things as they serve him here on earth. Paul was speaking about the struggle to do the right thing in a world that often entices us to do the wrong thing as he was writing to Christian friends at Ephesus in the first century, encouraging them to put on the breastplate of righteousness (Ephesians 6:14).

If we've come to know God as being the righteous God, revealed through His name as 'the LORD our righteousness', then we'll also have discovered that our righteousness is not ever going to be enough to make us acceptable to Him, and so He himself needs to become our righteousness – which is what He's made possible through the cross where Jesus, His Son, died for us. Then as we rejoice in this gift of righteousness which we simply receive through faith, God expects us to go on and by the help of His Spirit demonstrate God's righteous standards in contrast to the godless standards of our society. As the shepherd psalm reminds us: the Lord will guide us daily in paths of righteousness if we're prepared to let him take our hand and lead us.

Evidently this was a place on earth of which it could be said: 'the LORD is there'. Later God again indicated through Moses that there would be a place which he [God] would 'choose from all [their] tribes, to establish his name there for his dwelling' (Deuteronomy 12:5). The Jews understood that by saying His name would be established in the place of His choice, God was making clear that His presence would be associated with that place in a unique way. This was to be the only place to which they could bring their sacrifices to God as His people. Later when Jerusalem came to be identified as the place of God's choice, the place where King Solomon was to build a temple for God, Solomon himself reveled in this very idea – because he described the place of the temple as the place about which God had said "My name shall be there!" (2 Kings 8:29). That matches nicely with the expression we're studying: 'the LORD is there'. This actually tells us a lot about God and His purposes. The stupendous revelation is this: that from the beginning of time God has not only wanted a personal relationship with men and women, but He's also wanted to actually come and live among us on this earth – but at a place of His choice, and only with those who fulfil His conditions.

In the Old Testament, God's choice of Zion – as Jerusalem came to be called - is rather striking. "For the hill of Zion: Here I will dwell; for I have desired it" (Psalm 132:14). He was including in that statement His glorious purposes involving the Messiah and His presence on earth during the Millennium, the future reign of Christ on earth, when Zion will once again be central and far more glorious than ever before in history. After all, that's the setting, is it not, for Ezekiel's vision of a future city to be called by the name: 'the LORD is there'? There's even more than that to this idea of Zion as God's dwelling-place; there's more to this term "Zion" than meets the eye at first glance.

The Bible indicates that there's something in heaven – something in the very presence of God – of which Zion on earth was, and will be, a kind of reflection. There's a city in heaven which has, in a sense, cast its shadow on this earth. The city of Zion on earth was, and will be, a shadow, a representation, of the real city in heaven where God dwells. God's love for Zion above, Zion in heaven where His will is done, is such that it's led him to desire a representation or copy of it on this earth in every age – including in the future when Christ will reign and be acknowledged as supreme.

In every age, His desire has been to come and dwell on this earth among men and women whom He has brought together to do His will on earth as it is done in heaven. In every age, the earthly Zion or dwelling-place of God – whether we're thinking of a geographical city as in the Old Testament or a spiritual association of disciples designated as in the New Testament "House of God" – that dwelling place for God is modelled on the ultimate reality that's found in heaven itself. It's an earthly representation that can now be enjoyed collectively by those who take the Lord's commands seriously and give effect to them exactly as they were written by the Spirit of God two thousand years ago in what's known as 'the apostles' teaching'.

One of the apostles, Peter, draws the attention of New Testament readers to Zion, the city of God, when he wrote in his first letter:

"Coming to Him [Jesus] as to a living stone, rejected indeed by men, but chosen by God and precious, you also, as living stones, are being built up a spiritual house, a holy priesthood, to offer up spiritual sacrifices acceptable to God through Jesus Christ. Therefore it is also contained in the Scripture, "Behold, I lay in Zion a chief cornerstone, elect, precious, and he who believes on Him will by no means be put to shame." Therefore, to you who believe, He is precious" (1 Peter 2:4-7).

The reference Peter makes to Zion, the dwelling-place of God, is in connection with its earthly representation in the spiritual house for God today, made up of disciples of Jesus Christ who align themselves foursquare with the teaching of Christ – the Christ who's pictured as the foundation corner-stone. It's clear from the rest of Peter's letter that those he was writing to were born-again and baptized believers who were obeying the teaching Christ had delivered to His apostles and which is conveyed to us in the commands of the New Testament. Fulfilling the Lord's requirements in these things was, and remains, essential to satisfying the Father's longing for worshipers who would worship him "in spirit and in truth" as Jesus Himself explained to the woman that He met down at the well in the fourth chapter of John's gospel. Worship which is in spirit and in truth ties in with the realization that the true centre of our worship is in heavenly Zion – as the writer to the Hebrews also explains in chapter 12 of that letter:

"For you have not come to a mountain that can be
touched [and the writer was thinking about Mount
Sinai, the mountain associated with the ten com-
mandments] ... but you have come to Mount Zion
and to the city of the living God, the heavenly
Jerusalem ..." (Hebrews 12:18, 22).

This is to be the authentic worship experience of New Testament
Christians. Going back to Peter, he says it's precisely those who
keep on coming to the Lord in the heavenly Zion who are being
built up as a spiritual house on the earth. So, it would appear
that this realization is basic to achieving the purpose of God's
dwelling–place as represented on earth – the revelation that it's
ours to worship in Zion above where God is. God's
dwelling–place as represented on earth is the place of which it
can truly be said, 'the LORD is there'. Yes, the LORD is there,
and he wants us to be identified with Him there during this time
in which we're still obediently serving Him on this earth. It's
something the Bible says He desires, and He wants us to desire
it as well. Let's sum up by saying that it's really special to know
the psalmist's experience of having the Lord with us in our valley experiences, but the text we've connected with that, the verse
containing the revelation 'the LORD is there', invites us to go
even further into a present–day experience which we can share
in together with other disciples of Christ as we serve the Lord on
this earth – an experience of dwelling together where God himself dwells on this earth, reflecting the ultimate reality which is a
heavenly thing.

CHAPTER SEVEN: KNOWING GOD. . .AS OUR VICTORY BANNER

In his shepherd psalm David included the words, "you prepare a table before me in the presence of my enemies". The very mention of enemies links us to the place in the Bible where the expression 'the LORD is my banner' is found. This is the further revelation of God's personal name we'll be studying next. The place where we read about 'the LORD is my banner' is set during the time when the Israelites were making their way through the desert towards the Promised Land, after having been freed from Egypt. Here's part of that history, as it's found recorded in the book of Exodus 17:1-16 (NIV):

> "The whole Israelite community set out from the Desert of Sin, traveling from place to place as the LORD commanded. They camped at Rephidim, but there was no water for the people to drink. So they quarreled with Moses and said, "Give us water to drink." Moses replied, "Why do you quarrel with me? Why do you put the LORD to the test?" But the people were thirsty for water there, and they grumbled against Moses. They said, "Why did you bring us up out of Egypt to make us and our children and livestock die of thirst?" Then Moses cried out to the LORD, "What am I to do with these people? They are almost ready to stone me."

The LORD answered Moses, "Walk on ahead of the people. Take with you some of the elders of Israel and take in your hand the staff with which you struck the Nile, and go. I will stand there before you by the rock at Horeb. Strike the rock, and water will come out of it for the people to drink." So Moses did this in the sight of the elders of Israel. And he called the place Massah and Meribah because the Israelites quarreled and because they tested the LORD saying, "Is the LORD among us or not?" The Amalekites came and attacked the Israelites at Rephidim. Moses said to Joshua, "Choose some of our men and go out to fight the Amalekites. Tomorrow I will stand on top of the hill with the staff of God in my hands." So Joshua fought the Amalekites as Moses had ordered, and Moses, Aaron and Hur went to the top of the hill.

As long as Moses held up his hands, the Israelites were winning, but whenever he lowered his hands, the Amalekites were winning. When Moses' hands grew tired, they took a stone and put it under him and he sat on it. Aaron and Hur held his hands up – one on one side, one on the other – so that his hands remained steady till sunset. So Joshua overcame the Amalekite army with the sword. Then the LORD said to Moses, "Write this on a scroll as something to be remembered and make sure that Joshua hears it, because I will completely blot out the memory of Amalek from under heaven." Moses built an altar and called it The LORD is my Banner. He said, "For

hands were lifted up to the throne of the LORD. The
LORD will be at war against the Amalekites from
generation to generation."

The quarrelling and grumbling so prominent in this story is a sad
backdrop to a valuable lesson which contains this revelation that
the victory belongs to the LORD. Elsewhere the Bible assures us
that the battle is the LORD's, and this just confirms what ought
already to be implied by that – which is that the victory is surely also His. David, the author of Psalm 23, said in 1 Chroni-
cles 29:11: "yours, O Lord, is ... the victory." We're told that the
people were questioning, "Is the LORD among us, or not?" No
doubt the quarrelling and grumbling was due to the fact they'd
lost the sense of God's presence. If they'd been captivated, as they
ought to have been, with the awesome reality of the LORD's
presence being among them, surely there would have been no
grumbling in the ranks. How quickly the memory of God's mir-
acles in Egypt and at the Red Sea had become distant, receding
from them like a mirage in the desert. With rumbling stomachs
came grumbling tongues! God's presence had become a memory, not a reality. Perhaps they were selfishly demanding that God
should prove His presence by instantly gratifying their hunger
pangs. As the Lord Jesus said, it's an evil generation that seeks after signs.

They'd been privileged, the New Testament tells us, to eat spiritual food and to drink spiritual drink, but nevertheless with
most of them God was not well-pleased (1 Corinthians 10:4-5).
We, too, can eat the bread and drink the wine in remembrance
of our Lord each Sunday and still not be in a spiritual condition
that pleases the Lord. These Bible stories were written to serve

us warning. Maybe it was the grumbling which distracted them, but somehow they let down their guard. The enemy crept up behind them unawares. The book of Exodus doesn't tell us this, but Deuteronomy 25:17 describes how they came up at the rear and destroyed the stragglers. It was a satanically orchestrated attack. This kind of sneaky tactic reminds us of the Devil's strategies. It's just so typical of his wiles which unsettle us in our weaker, off-guard moments and they often attack us with negative things born of fleshly jealousy. But just who were these enemies in the Exodus story? They were the Amalekites; people descended from the profane and godless Esau (Genesis 36:11). God here promises to have war with them from generation to generation, until we find them finally destroyed by David in 1 Samuel 30. As David destroyed the Amalekites, so it was David's greater Son who finally broke Satan's power at the cross.

Speaking of Jesus links us into the first Bible mention of Joshua. Jesus is the same name after passing through at least a couple of different languages. The name Jesus or Joshua or Y'shua means 'Yah (the LORD) is salvation'. It brings us right back to the name of God that we're tracking in this book. But it's Joshua, Moses' eventual successor, who's the deliverer here - wielding his sword at the head of a hand-picked bunch of warriors in the valley. If we can use our imagination, observe these swordsmen in the valley through the lens of a camera or telescope, panning upwards to the mountain top at the valley-side. Stop when you reach three figures silhouetted against the skyline. In the centre of this trio is Moses with the rod of God in his hand, that rod through which God worked His wonders.

As Moses holds this staff skywards, the people of God are turning the tide on the valley-floor. Then, as we watch, we see Moses tire and see the staff in his hands sink slowly earthwards. Now the enemy is once again gaining the upper-hand down in the valley. God was teaching them – and us – that the outcome of the battle was not determined by lifting up the sword in the valley below, but by raising up the staff on the hilltop. The victory was not carved out by the sword, but it was granted by divine instrumentality. So it is in anything we struggle with. The power of prayer is the decisive factor, as symbolised here in the upheld rod, even the staff of God which Moses was helped by Aaron and Hur to hold aloft. Like Moses, we, too, need help for we're beset by the feebleness of our nature – even as Moses wearied and let down his hands.

Like Moses, we have two helpers who intercede for us in the all-important matter of prayer (Romans 8:26,34). They are the Holy Spirit and the Lord Jesus. Their work for us in relation to prayer is described for us in that wonderful eighth chapter of the letter to the Romans. Let's encourage ourselves to raise the profile of prayer in our lives of service for the Lord. Prayerlessness brings defeat; but prayerfulness leads to victory. In recognition of the fact that the victory was the LORD's doing, Moses built an altar and called it, "The LORD is my banner"; a victory banner.

It's the verse after that which is really interesting. In some English versions, it reads, 'The LORD has sworn' (about His intention to wage war on Amalek from generation to generation). More literally it reads, 'There's a hand on the throne of Yah' or even 'a hand raised up against the throne'. The issue in the mind of translators has been whose hand is it that's being referred to here? If it's the LORD's hand, then it must mean that he's vowing to destroy Amalek. If it's Moses' hand, then it stresses our part in prayer and our lifting up holy hands to God in prayer (as we are commanded to do in 1 Timothy 2:8). But if it's Satan's hand that's seen here as raised against God's throne, then we're reminded of the opposition we face.

But how good it is to be reminded that victory is assured against our enemy. We may lose a battle here and there, but the war is won, because it – and the victory - belongs to the LORD. This is surely one of the precious revelations surrounding God's personal name, the name of Yahweh. Even in the ebb and flow of life's experiences, those who belong to Yahweh know that victory is secure. We're not working towards victory as though it could yet elude us, but we're working from victory, the victory of Jesus Christ forever sealed at the cross. One day the Lord Jesus will destroy the last enemy, death, and all things will be placed forever under those victorious nail-pierced feet of His. When He brings us into His banqueting house and prepares a table before us, we'll know the full truth of the children's chorus: 'His banner over me is love'.

CHAPTER EIGHT: KNOWING GOD...AS THE SANCTIFIER

We're all familiar, I'm sure, with the opening words of the Lord's prayer. '(Our) Father (in heaven) hallowed be Your name' (Luke 11:2). To hallow means to sanctify or treat as holy. Any approach that we make to God in prayer must account for the fact that He is holy and so we say 'hallowed be Your name'. God's name is revealed in the Old Testament as Yahweh, His personal name. He shares it with us for He intends men and women at all times to discover a personal relationship with Himself, the great God of heaven. That's amazing when you think about it.

Imagine if some bearer of high office in the world singled you or me out as an individual and said just call me "Barack" or "Elizabeth", or whatever their name was. But the God who shares or manifests His name with us so that we can know Him by His grace, at the very same time reminds us that reverent intimacy must never be confused with careless familiarity. There's a section towards the back of the third Bible book of Leviticus which is sometimes referred to as 'the holiness code'. It's a detailed section that regulated the behaviour of the Israelites when they were called to be God's people. It's in this section that we find another aspect of God's name. In Leviticus chapter 20, verse 8, God told His people: 'I am the LORD (Yahweh) who sanctifies you'.

He went on to give instructions for people and priest alike, spelling out what holiness meant in every-day terms. The priests were, of course, sanctified through the anointing oil when they were initially consecrated or set apart for priestly service. Psalm

23, you'll remember, talks about anointing with oil, and that becomes the 'peg' in the Psalm on which we can hang this particular revelation associated with God's name.

We now return to the holiness section of Leviticus again where God says: 'I am the LORD (Yahweh) who sanctifies you'. The whole point of this section was to make clear that if they were the people of God, the holy God of heaven, then they'd have to be holy themselves - they'd have to be seen to be different from the other nations surrounding them with their defiling practices. In fact, God had earlier laid it on the line to them: "Be holy, for I am holy" (Leviticus 11:44-45). That was then, but what about now? Well, God hasn't changed, and the New Testament, through the apostle Peter, repeats God's command to believers on the Lord Jesus: "Be holy as I am holy" (1 Peter 1:16). So this is one of the basic revelations about God. Whenever we're tempted to treat sin lightly, this is what we're losing sight of – the holiness of God. What we must learn about God, and learn well, is that God is holy. If we have entered into a personal relationship with this holy God through faith in Jesus Christ by the grace of God, then the Bible has two things to say to us on the theme of our topic today.

The first is that we have been made holy. It's something God did for us the moment we first turned from our sin and our sinfulness and put our full weight of truth in the "Son of God who loved me and gave himself for me", as Paul described his own experience in Galatians 2:20. At that moment, by virtue of Christ's sacrifice, God made us holy in Christ. He now continues to see us in and through Christ, and that means He sees us as holy as His Son! The Bible in fact calls the true believer on the Lord Jesus a "saint". Centuries of religious history has confused the meaning of this word for many people. But getting right back to Bible reality and truth, a saint simply means a 'saved sinner' – someone who's now 'set apart' in Jesus Christ. It happens through faith when God calls us through the Gospel, so we read about being 'called to be saints' in 1 Corinthians 1:2. No religious order or institution appoints saints, but God, the holy God, calls them into existence by His pure grace.

As a believer in Jesus Christ nothing can change the fact that we're made holy in God's sight. The perfect holiness of Christ with which God has clothed us can never be tainted, the work of the cross will remain effective for ever for all who believe. But there's also a practical dimension which can sometimes be confused with this in the minds of some. There's certainly an obligation on those who know God to live holy lives. But we need to distinguish between character and behaviour. God has for ever dealt with the matter of our character through the cross of Jesus. It's all through faith by His grace. But our behaviour in this life as Christians is another matter altogether. What God has done for us in this connection is that he's given us His Holy Spirit so that we have the power to live a holy life.

God does not, of course, ask the impossible of us. He gives us the power to live as He commands. It's His intention that our daily lives, our behaviour, will display to others the new, holy inner character we have from God. So that's the second thing we referred to earlier. Remember we said there were two things that follow from the revelation that God is holy? The first we discovered was this: that all Christian believers have been made holy as to their character – as to their new identity in Christ. But, secondly, Christian believers must become holy as to their behaviour in this world. Our behaviour sadly can disguise our character but thankfully - since it's by God's grace – it can't change or in any way affect it or spoil it. Christ's own work cannot be spoiled or made ineffective, and that's what our new character as Christians depends upon. This understanding ought to give us the liberty and incentive to live holy lives to God's glory. We've mentioned Peter's writing earlier, and already mentioned the Lord's prayer. So let's round off with more words of Peter which use the same word 'hallow' or 'sanctify':

"... sanctify Christ as Lord in your hearts, always being ready to make a defence to everyone who asks you to give an account for the hope that is in you, yet with gentleness and reverence; and keep a good conscience so that in the thing in which you are slandered, those who revile your good behavior in Christ may be put to shame" (1 Peter 3:15-16 NASB).

Peter was encouraging these Jewish Christians to set apart Christ as Lord in their heart. The word 'Lord' refers back to the Yahweh of the Old Testament (since the quote is an adaptation of Isaiah 8:13). So they were being encouraged to hallow their Messiah, the Lord Jesus, as Yahweh God in their hearts. This verse, among so many, underlines for us the deity of the Lord Jesus. It's also interesting that these Christian Jews weren't only to find a refuge in Christ Jesus as they set Him apart as Lord of their lives, but they were to be ready to give an answer to these persecutors who attacked them and the Word of God which they believed.

The words 'give an account' are the translation of a word which at the time was used as a legal term in the law courts. It literally means 'to talk off from' and was used of an attorney who talked his client off from a charge. He did this by presenting a verbal defence. So we're encouraged here to talk the Bible off from any charges people make against it - a verbal defence against the Bible's critics who would like to charge it with containing errors of different kinds. However, we're to make our defence with gentleness and reverence. This will be the inevitable result if we've truly sanctified Christ as Lord (LORD) in our hearts. For if we regard the Lord Christ as our Protector and we fear or reverence him, then we'll not be afraid of any mere man who sets out to criticize the Bible. We'll do it all with gentleness and reverence because the LORD is holy and He is our Sanctifier.

CHAPTER NINE: KNOWING GOD...AS SHEPHERD

In our final chapter, let's recap how we've been relating the various 'Jehovah' titles of God to different parts of Psalm 23, known as the Shepherd psalm. We began with the opening words, 'the LORD is my shepherd, I shall not want' – to which we attached the statement: 'the LORD will provide'. With the restful imagery conjured up by the words: "He makes me to lie down in green pastures; he leads me beside the still waters", we next associated the idea of 'the LORD is peace'. Then 'The LORD your healer' connected with "He restores my soul". Whereas "he leads me in the paths of righteousness for His name's sake" brought us in thought to 'the LORD our righteousness'.

Following that came, "Yea, though I walk through the valley of the shadow of death, I will fear no evil; for You are with me" - which we took as a reminder of the fact that 'the LORD is (right) there' with us. The expression 'the LORD is my banner', we felt, was all about celebrating a victory, which we laid alongside the words, "You prepare a table before me in the presence of my enemies". And finally, the words, "you anoint my head with oil" can remind us of the fact that 'the LORD is the One who sanctifies' – at least it did so as we recalled how prophets, priests and kings long ago in Israel were set apart for their sacred service through being anointed with the sanctifying oil of God.

So, following the order of Psalm 23, we worked our way through the remarkable way in which God has revealed His name to us and in revealing His personal name, of course, he's disclosed the kind of character that's very uniquely His. That's why we called this book 'Knowing God'. I do hope we'll get to know and serve God better as a result of having studied these marvelous declarations in which God has showed us what he's really like. In bringing this study to a conclusion, I think it's right that we spend a little while considering the opening words of Psalm 23 themselves: "The LORD is my shepherd". After all, they're really another revelation of God – telling us about His shepherd character. He's the one who truly cares for us, and, if we let Him, He'll always be our guide. Those opening five words of Psalm 23 – "the LORD is my shepherd" always remind me of the story of a shepherd-boy in Switzerland.

One day he was sitting high up on one of the Alps, playing a simple kind of flute. The sheep around him were enjoying the soft grass. Into this picturesque scene with its nearby glaciers came a holiday-maker, making his way up the narrow mountain path. He greeted the shepherd-boy and enquired what his name was. "Henry," the boy replied. "Well you can just call me Uncle Hans," said the holiday-maker, and went on to ask what the boy was doing. The ten-year-old informed Uncle Hans that he was on school holiday and had been given the job of looking after his father's sheep. "I see," Hans said. "I guess that makes you a young shepherd then! Tell me," he went on, "have you ever heard about the Good Shepherd?" "Sir," Henry quickly replied, "I'm a good shepherd because I try my best when looking after my father's sheep."

"Oh, I'm sure you do," the holiday maker said. "That makes you a good shepherd, but I was asking if you knew the Good Shepherd." He went on to explain to young Henry that the Good

Shepherd is a title that belongs to the Lord Jesus, the Son of God who came from heaven to earth to die on a cross. "He's living again," Uncle Hans said, "and he's the Good Shepherd who brings all the sheep who belong to him to his Father's house in heaven." Hans explained that Jesus' sheep were his followers. And he added, "There's nothing better than knowing the Lord Jesus." At that point young Henry asked if Jesus could make sure he, too, was safely brought to the Father's house in heaven. "Why, of course," Uncle Hans replied, "but there's something that needs to happen first. Have you ever done anything wrong, Henry?"

"Sure," Henry admitted, looking a little ashamed when he added that he'd already been a bit naughty that very week. "Well, then," Hans said, "You first need to ask him to forgive you for all your sins. If you do that in a simple prayer to him, then he'll take your sins away, because that's the reason why he suffered and died on the cross – it was to pay the price for your forgiveness; for the forgiveness of all who call upon him as their Saviour."

There and then, on the mountainside, with that little encouragement from Uncle Hans, Henry knelt down and prayed a simple prayer to receive the Lord Jesus. Uncle Hans had no doubt that it was sincerely done, and so he taught Henry a Bible text. It was Psalm 23 verse 1, just the first five words: "The LORD is my shepherd" - a very relevant text for the young shepherd boy! To impress it upon him, Hans encouraged Henry to associate each of its five words with one of the fingers of his hand. As he said, "The LORD is my shepherd," he pointed to each of Henry's fingers in turn. But he specially emphasized the fourth word, 'my' – and he encouraged Henry to grip his ring finger with his other

had when he came to that word. In this way, Hans left the youngster in no doubt that anyone who did as he's done anyone who
had turned from their sins and believed in the Lord Jesus could
truthfully say, "The LORD is my shepherd".

Hans checked up on Henry a couple times afterwards, but soon
the holiday period was over, and Henry was back at school. Soon
it was winter, a time of year which has its dangers in a Swiss
village among the mountains: dangers like avalanches, when a
great mass of snow slides down the mountainside and sometimes
buries entire houses under its weight. One afternoon when Henry came home from school, he found his father waiting for him.
His dad looked a bit worried, and Henry soon learnt this was because his mum had been taken ill. The doctor had been and left a
prescription, but someone needed to go and collect the medicine
from the next village which was half an hour's walk away. Henry
agreed to go at once, while his dad stayed at home with his mum.

Everything was fine until he was returning with the bottle of
medicine in his jacket pocket. It suddenly became quite dark.
Soon there was a deafening noise, like thunder. Except it wasn't
thunder, it was an avalanche and it was headed for the path Henry was on. There was nowhere to run, even if there had been
time. There wasn't, and soon the avalanche buried him and the
path. The villagers had heard the noise, of course. Henry's father raised the alarm after telephoning the pharmacy and dis-
covering that Henry would have been on his way back when
the avalanche happened. The villagers took their spades and dug
along the length of the path - at last they found him under the
snow. He was cold and dead. But they were puzzled by the fact
that one of his hands was holding the fourth finger, the ring-fin-

ger of his other hand. Henry's father understood at once what it meant for Henry had told him all about Uncle Hans and how he'd learnt to say, "The LORD is my shepherd" by reciting it on his fingers.

Henry's dad now realized Henry had seen the danger, had known he couldn't escape it, and, thinking at that moment of the Lord Jesus who would bring his sheep safely to his Father's house above, he'd gripped his fourth finger as if to say, "my"- "The LORD is my shepherd." And that was how they'd discovered him. His parents found comfort in knowing their young son was now in heaven with his Saviour, the Good Shepherd who himself had laid down his life for his sheep. As we've related each one of the revelations of the LORD's name to the Shepherd Psalm, perhaps the best summary of all we've shared will be if each of us can say, "The LORD is my shepherd."

BONUS BOOK: GOD'S ABUNDANCE FOR OUR SUFFICIENCY

CHAPTER ONE: SPIRITUAL SUFFICIENCY IN OUR SERVICE

The guests at table were finishing their meal when they were taken by surprise. Whatever could the little boy mean? He'd just asked if he could have 'some fishint'. The hostess scratched her head - some what? She was puzzled by this request, until it dawned on her that only a minute or two earlier she had asked everyone if they had had 'sufficient' to eat. All the adults had gratefully replied 'yes' - leaving the youngster to think that he'd missed out on something!

In this little book, we're going to focus on Paul's second Bible letter to the Corinthians. We will trace a couple of important words in that letter which was written to the early Church of God at Corinth. One of those is the little boy's word: 'sufficient'. Paul uses it in three separate sections of his letter - and it seems to me as though we could label the things he talks about as spiritual sufficiency, financial sufficiency and physical sufficiency. Another word that appears again and again (in various forms) is the word 'abundance' or 'abounding'. Proverbs 28:20 says that a faithful person shall abound with blessings. Have you ever tried to count your many blessings, as the old hymn suggests? You can't do it, can you? There are simply too many.

That's exactly what 'abundance' means: something that's 'beyond measure'. If you use a modern translation of the Bible you might not find the word 'abundance', but you'll certainly find lots of expressions like 'immeasurable' or 'beyond measure'. As you read though Second Corinthians, you'll find that God's grace and comfort are among the things that are said to abound. And when we want to look for more abounding things, we need to look no further than Christian joy and love, which have their source in God, of course.

It all seems designed to teach us - through the experiences recorded in this letter - that Gods abundance is for our sufficiency - and that's something that holds good in our service, in our stewardship and in our sufferings. Let's begin our look at the first of these: God's abundance for our sufficiency in our spiritual service. As early as chapter two and verse fifteen we read:

> "We are to God the fragrance of Christ among those who are being saved and among those who are perishing. To the one we are the aroma of death leading to death, and to the other the aroma of fife leading to life. And who is sufficient for these things?"

This is our introduction to our subject of sufficiency - and it's in the context of reaching out to others with God's good news. The question: 'Who is sufficient for these things?' is associated with telling the good news of Jesus - and no wonder! Who hasn't met with apathy or, worse, antagonism, when attempting to share something of God's great love with family, friends, colleagues or neighbours? I can remember times spent taking the gospel from door to door when the whole time seemed to be without a single positive reaction.

Yet so often, as one door closes another opens. That had been Paul's experience, too, and he traced God's leading in it - always leading him in triumph in Christ (v.14). So to his own question: 'Who is sufficient for these things?', Paul gives the resounding answer in chapter 3 verse 5 that 'our sufficiency is from God'. Let's read exactly what he says: "Not that we are sufficient of ourselves to think of anything as being from ourselves, but our sufficiency is from God, who also made us sufficient as ministers of the new covenant."

So this is spiritual sufficiency - a sufficiency in, and for, our service for God - God making us sufficient as ministers of the new covenant, and doing it out of His own abounding grace. To explain how it works, Paul contrasts Moses' work for God long ago with our evangelism in new covenant times - since the death of Christ, in other words. Moses once (in Numbers 11:14) said to God: 'I am not able to bear all these people alone'. Since the number of the people he'd led out of Egypt might have been anything up to two million in number, he was absolutely right. God never expected Moses to bear all these people by himself. Paul had learned the secret when he said: "I can do all things through Christ who strengthens me" (Philippians 4:13).

How often we tend to rely on ourselves instead of on the Lord! Let's try to learn Paul's secret of knowing God's abundance rather than our own self-sufficiency - and to begin by going back to his reference to Moses in chapter 3. Remember how Moses used to put a veil over his face after meeting with God? The skin of his face used to shine from his having been in the presence of God. But with time that reflected glory faded and the veil he was wearing prevented the people seeing that decreasing glory. Why does Paul remind us of this? Well, he's teaching us that when we were sill unsaved we also had a veil - not over our face, but our heart - a veil which hindered us from seeing the Saviour. But, in the working of God's Spirit, that veil was removed at the time of our conversion. And the removal of this restriction is the work of the Holy Spirit - he's the one who gives us freedom.

Paul writes: 'When one turns to the Lord, the veil is taken away. Now the Lord is the Spirit; and where the Spirit of the Lord is, there is liberty' - that's verse 17 of 2 Corinthians 3. This liberty is something that's often misunderstood. It seems the weirdest things are sometimes done under the pretext of being 'in the Spirit'. But the liberating work of the Holy Spirit here is a process of change which He works in us - a change towards Christlikeness - which at the same time will be a change away from self-sufficiency. The Spirit works to free us from relying on ourselves.

Chapter 4 verse 6 says: "God ... commanded light to shine out of darkness, who has shone in our hearts to give the light of the knowledge of the glory of God in the face of Jesus Christ." Just as the people looked on Moses' face long ago, we're to look upon the Lord's face. How do we do that? It's by reading the Bible, and the Lord being revealed to us through it. Christ is revealed to us by the illumination of the Spirit.

Even that's not change as such - there's more - more than being revealed to us, God's purpose is for Christ to be revealed 'in' us as we become not just illuminated, but imitators of Christ. Chapter 3:18 says: "we all, with unveiled face, beholding as in a mirror the glory of the Lord, are being transformed into the same image from glory to glory, just as by the Spirit of the Lord". The mirror is the Word of God which we look into to see the glory of the Lord. It's by 'beholding that we're transformed - a liberating change from self-sufficiency into Christlikeness. In the process, we become more aware of God's abundant sufficiency for our service.

But it's a gradual process, and when our thirst for the Lord and His Word are not what they could be it gets hindered - but how wonderful that it's a change 'from glory to glory'. I wouldn't want to swap places with Moses in this respect - for his experience was of a decreasing glory, as the shining of his face faded away over time. What's open to us is the experience of an increasing glory - increasing Christlikeness - changed by one glorious degree to another. It is not hard to see how all this relates to the original context of evangelism. As more of the attractiveness of Christ is seen in our lives, it will surely have the effect of others being attracted to Him though us - and all by the sufficiency that's from God! By people reading the gospel in our lives, when we become the 'living epistles' Paul's been speaking about earlier in the same chapter, we really can be effective in our service as 'ministers of the new covenant' - even when we come up against pressures, disappointments and opposition just like Paul and his co-workers faced in this letter. Like them, we can overcome by His abundance of grace, comfort, love and joy.

CHAPTER TWO: FINANCIAL SUFFICIENCY IN OUR STEWARDSHIP

'God's abundance for our sufficiency' is our subject, and it's taken from Paul's second letter to the Corinthians. In this chapter, we're going to be focusing on sufficiency in stewardship and we will be looking into chapters 8 and 9, if you have your Bible handy. Paul starts by saying to the believers at Corinth: 'We make known to you the grace of God bestowed on the churches of Macedonia: that in a great trial of affliction the abundance of their joy and their deep poverty abounded in the riches of the liberality."

In a sense, we're beginning where we left off our look at 'sufficiency in service': on the theme of Christlikeness. The generosity of the Macedonians in their stewardship gives us a very clear glimpse of Christ in them. Isn't it delightful that here, where we get one of the most precious revelations of the grace of the Lord Jesus, it's occasioned by the generous giving of these Macedonian believers? The grace of God in them had bought them to full surrender, seen in giving themselves to the Lord. The affliction that they had experienced had only served to intensify their joy. In the midst of their deep poverty, they were able to display great generosity. Surrender, joy and generosity: these characteristics in their lives turn our attention to the Lord Jesus. The grace of the one man, Jesus Christ (Romans 5) produced perfect lifelong surrender to the will of His God and Father. Even though, as the psalms had predicted, He was afflicted from His youth up, Hiss surrender wasn't accompanied by grim determination. No, the joy of the Lord was His strength as He headed onwards to the cross. The One who borrowed a manger, a boat, a penny, a donkey and a tomb, was the same One who never sent anyone away empty.

So, we owe a great debt to the Macedonians - for their obedient confession of the gospel of Christ - because their outstanding generosity brings us the verse about 'the grace of our Lord Jesus Christ, that though He was rich, yet for your sakes He became poor, that you through His poverty might become rich.' I hope it whets our appetite so that in our lives, too, Christ might be clearly expressed. On the matter of stewardship, it's quite a challenge to ask ourselves if we're at the Macedonian level of giving or at the Corinthian level. The Corinthians were full of good intentions but were a bit backward when it came to actually going through with it.

By contrast, the Macedonians were gracious givers. Paul writes of the grace of God that had been given in the churches of Macedonia - and that grace was their spirit of generosity. They abounded in that grace unlike the Corinthians (see 8:7). True, the Corinthians abounded in other things like faith and knowledge, but they hadn't yet appreciated that generous stewardship is a mark of Christian character. Generous giving to the Lord is an evidence of God's transforming work in our hearts - a change towards Christlikeness and away from self-sufficiency. It's no coincidence that it is these Macedonian believers, transformed to be like Christ, who model for us the reality of God's sufficiency in stewardship. Despite the fact that they themselves didn't have much of this world's goods, they reflected God's own generous, giving nature by being more concerned for others than for themselves.

It was in this that they gave a practical demonstration of their likeness to Christ. He gave Himself, and He gave entirely. He gave voluntarily, and He gave willingly. So did the Macedonians. In forfeiting much-needed cash, they made life harder for themselves, and in this sacrificial sense they gave themselves to the Lord. It wasn't just the money they gave, but it was also the comfort and relief they could have bought with it had they not given it. They willingly made a personal sacrifice by depriving themselves; and the deprivation was real enough, for we read of their deep poverty.

It's precisely this readiness to give that's stressed in verses 11 and 12 of chapter 8 as one of the great principles of our stewardship; Paul says to the Corinthians: "but now you must complete the doing of it; that as there was a readiness to desire it, so there also may be a completion out of what you have. For if there is first a willing mind, it is accepted according to what one has, and not according to what he does not have." Our readiness to forfeit the full personal benefit of our income is the measure of the manifestation of this grace of giving in our experience. Let's explore further the link between God's abundance and our sufficiency in stewardship by turning our attention to 2 Corinthians chapter 9 verses 8 to 10:

> "And God as able to make all grace abound toward you, that you, always having all sufficiency in all things, may have an abundance for every good work. As it is written: "He has dispersed abroad, He has

given to the poor; Hs righteousness endures forever."
Now may He who supplies seed to the sower, and
bread for food, supply and multiply the seed you have
sown and increase the fruits of your righteousness."

We sing about God's 'amazing grace', don't we? But these verses
are talking about God's abounding grace! This is certainly the
source of our sufficiency in stewardship. The word 'sufficiency'
was actually used, wasn't it? God's Word spoke about our 'always
having all sufficiency in all things'. Its every bit as clear in chapter
9 regarding our stewardship as it was in chapter 3 regarding our
service that our sufficiency is from God. What abundance lies
behind this sufficiency! Think about it once more: ALWAYS
having ALL sufficiency in ALL things. Not sometimes in some
things, but always in all things. Wonderful as this is, let's not get
carried away with some false idea that God's plan is for Him to
be forever indulging His children. These verses are much loved
by present-day advocates of the so-called 'prosperity gospel'
which says: 'God wants you to be rich'.

This is not a promise that if we give to God, then He'll give us
back much more wealth for our own ends. The sense here is that
if we sow sparingly (if we don't give much) we'll not be instru-
mental in bringing much blessing to the lives of others. Bounti-
ful givers will reap, in the sense that their giving will bear fruit in
the lives of the recipients. It is totally out of character to see this
passage as in any way supporting self-seeking giving. The intention is to bless others, to look for a great harvest of blessing in the
lives of others, and not for our own financial reward.

God promises to provide our sufficiency out of His abundance -
always, in everything - so that we, in turn, might bless others gen-
erously. Paul says: 'may He who supplies seed to the sower, and
bread for food, supply and multiply the seed you have sown and
increase the fruits of your righteousness'. In other words, God's
sufficient supply to us serves to fulfill two things. First of all, He
gives 'bread for food': that's God's supply for our own domes-
tic requirements. For we need to maintain an efficient lifestyle
ourselves in order to be effective in service. Our heavenly Father
knows this and supplies every need of ours 'according to Hs riches in glory by Christ Jesus' (see Philippians chapter 4).

Secondly, as mentioned here, God, as well as giving 'bread for
food', also gives 'seed for sowing'. Perhaps this is a stranger form
of words and we need to take a little more time over it. In this
section, giving to God is called 'sowing'. It might be meeting
someone else's material needs as part of our 'stewardship'. God
promises, in His abounding grace, to supply us, not only with
'bread for food' to cater for our own modest needs, but to bless
us with the means to make contributions and donations wherev-
er necessary. If we do this, as intended, rather than hoarding up
the surplus for ourselves, we'll 'abound in every good work'. So
despite all that the 'prosperity preachers' tell us, when God mul-
tiplies our seed it's not for hoarding, but for sowing, in order to
reap a harvest of blessing in the lives of others.

Lastly, there are two words in this section worth a mention –
they are 'bountifully' and 'liberality'. In some versions at least,
the donation coming from the Corinthians is spoken of as their
'bounty' (9:5). That literally means a 'spoken benediction'. It reminds us that what we give is more than what its worth in purely

financial terms, it is a token of our conferred goodwill; it's an expression of love. We bless with our gifts.

The other word, 'liberality', has the idea of 'singleness'. At first, the idea of singleness seems totally unrelated to the business of giving. But Jesus taught that no-one can serve two masters: certainly not God and money. 'Singleness' in this sense means freedom from the double-mindedness that would taint our giving with selfish motivation. When we give 'with singleness' we're not looking for a pay-off ourselves.

CHAPTER THREE: PHYSICAL SUFFICIENCY IN OUR SUFFERINGS

We're still exploring Second Corinthians under the theme of 'God's abundance for our sufficiency'. It's a theme that suggests itself directly from Scripture because, in three separate sections in this letter by Paul, he uses the word 'sufficiency ' in the context of His abounding comfort and grace and His abounding love and joy. The key passage we come to now is in 2 Corinthians 12 where Paul, it seems, shares something of a vision he'd had. He spoke of how he was caught up into Paradise and heard 'exalted words' and then he goes on in verse 7 to explain that to prevent him being 'exalted above measure by the abundance of the revelations' a thorn in the flesh was given to him. He says "concerning this thing I pleaded with the Lord three times that it might depart from me. And He said to me, "My grace is sufficient for you, for My strength is made perfect in weakness.'"

This is really quite a fascinating insight into God's dealings with Hs servant, including how it shows that God's sovereign purposes allow and use hindrances that Satan harnesses in our lives. Satan really has the power to affect our physical well-being and what he does is calculated to be harmful. But God is over all, setting the limits and using for our greater good whatever Satan maliciously intends. Some have thought that Paul's physical handicap was poor eyesight, judging from what he said about the Galatians (4:15) that they would have plucked out their own eyes and done him a swap. Perhaps, however, it's left vague deliberately so that we can relate any of our chronic complaints to it. Whatever it may have been, it's clear that the blessing that flowed from this was Paul's humility.

It's hard not to make a comparison with the story of Job. Remember how God allowed Satan to wreak havoc with Job? His possessions, family and personal health were plundered or destroyed. This happened, not because Job was sinning, but because he was righteous. God knew what Job was made of whereas Satan had him figured all wrong. If you read the 42 chapters that are devoted to this one individual's suffering, you'll never read that it was ever revealed to Job why he had to go through all that pain. What's clear, however, is that he emerged from this test with a much greater sense of God. "I have heard of You by the hearing of the ear, but now my eye sees You" (Job 42:5). That changed attitudes and perspectives can be more satisfying than answers and instant relief seems to be the message of the book of Job.

That's also the way Paul viewed it. He spoke about preferring to "take pleasure in infirmities, in reproaches, in needs, in persecutions, in distresses, for Christ's sake". It's as though he got to the point where he says that he wouldn't have done without the discomfort, since that would have meant also doing without the grace and sense of God's sufficiency. This is the God who, thirty-one times in the book of Job, is described by the title 'Shaddai' - which basically means 'sufficiency'. The message is: God is our sufficiency. Out of God's abounding grace, Job and Paul found a real sense of sufficiency, sustaining them through physical suffering.

Not all of us, thankfully, are called upon to suffer anything like as much as Job or Paul; but equally, because we live in a fallen world, we'll never be completely immune from pain and discomfort. Romans chapter 8 describes our situation by saying that the whole creation groans in pain and even we groan within ourselves. This groaning is the result of God having subjected this world to a curse: the very one we can read about in the first book of the Bible. Corruption and decay were not part of the original design of the universe. They came about when God subjected the creation to futility as a judgment upon our first parents' disobedience.

There's a sense in which we all suffer as a result of the curse of Genesis chapter 3 - with a pain that's not always physical, but very real. In a fallen world, hurts and disappointments are inevitable. How do we respond to them? One way people react is by denying them, or seeking to defend against them at all costs. Perhaps, they think these things shouldn't happen to a committed Christian and so they struggle with guilt feelings. Yet God hasn't promised us physical comfort now, and Paul acknowledged these things in his life, and went so far as to rejoice in them. According to his testimony, they worked in him to make his passion for Christ more acute. Why is it that pain and frustration are unavoidable? Let me remind you of our early history.

We were made in the image of God, Genesis tells us. That included the ability to be creative; perhaps at first expressed in the way Adam cultivated and kept the Garden of Eden, for that was the specific task allotted to him. Next, we read about God's verdict on Adam when He said in Genesis 2: "It is not good that man should be alone". In other words we were designed for partnership - and so Eve was formed. The highlight of their time in the Garden must have been when they knew the presence and voice of the Lord God as He came to meet and walk with them in the cool of the day. We were built for fellowship with our Maker. Now, because of the way we've been created, it's only natural for each of us to want to be comfortable and enjoy the satisfaction of a job well done. It's equally natural to long for the pleasure of excellent relationships and for deep spiritual experiences with God.

But also, because of the fact that this world was cursed though our first parents' rebellion, it's natural for us, in a now fallen and imperfect world, to groan with the pain of disappointment when things don't go well, when relationships sour and whenever we feel far away from God. After all, we weren't designed for ground with weeds, for relationships with strains and for fellowship with interruptions. Ever since Eden, we have thirsted for the way things were at the very beginning.

The Bible recognizes our thirst. In Jeremiah 2:13 we hear God saying: "My people have committed two evils: they have forsaken Me, the fountain of living waters, and hewn themselves cisterns - broken cisterns that can hold no water." Often, like Israel, we try to satisfy our thirst by our own independent, self-sufficient strategies. For example, when we suffer disappointment in some relationship quite early in life, we feel pain and we instinctively demand pain relief. We decide we're not going to allow ourselves to be hurt that way again. Gradually and subtly, we develop a self-protecting way of relating to other people. It may be that my efficiency is my way of preventing close, tender relationships forming, because I know they leave me vulnerable to being hurt.

Or it may be that my shyness is my way of avoiding embarrassment and loss of image. If I've once known the pain of feeling rejected, the chances are I'll not risk letting anyone know what I'm really like for fear that then they wouldn't want to know me. All that is an attempt to be self-sufficient in dealing with the rejections and pain that are inevitable for anyone in a fallen world. In other words, by using strategies like these (the 'broken cisterns' to use the prophet's words) I'm putting my own interests first; I'm loving myself more than anyone else. Basically, the Bible says that's wrong behavior. That's manipulation, not ministry. That's not what Paul was all about. He'd known more than his fair share of things appearing to go wrong - of disappointment in relationships with co-workers for example - and in Romans chapter 7 he talks candidly of spiritual failure and wretchedness. But he'd grasped the secret of deep trust in God's gracious sufficiency though it all: depending on God's sufficiency, and not on his own strategy.

How can we know this type of sufficiency? Perhaps Paul would say that we first need to face up to our disappointments, feel the pain and let the pain drive us to God. Surely it was precisely Paul's thirst that whetted his passion for Christ - to the point of even finding pleasure in pain though the richer experience of the Lord to which it bought him. When the Lord Jesus promised 'living water' to thirsty people in John 4:10 and 7:37, He wasn't promising the removal of all disappointments (not yet, at least - that belongs to Heaven), but He was offering hope whenever we hurt. It's thirst-quenching whenever we remind ourselves of the value God puts on each one of us, when we remember that we're loved by Him with a love we can never lose, and especially when we realize that there's something significant planned by God for each one of us to do for Him.

As we allow God's grace to change us to become deeply dependent on His sufficiency, we find ourselves set free to truly love, even when we're hurting. We all want successful careers, loving partners, money and well-behaved children; but if and when they don't materialize, we need not be crushed if we bring the thirst of our legitimate longings, and the hurt of our painful disappointments, to the Lord. By His grace, we trust and hope in Him at a deep level for His sufficiency.

Did you love *Knowing God - Reflections on Psalm 23*? Then you should read *After God's Own Heart : The Life of David* by Brian Johnston!

International Bible teacher and radio broadcaster Brian Johnston helps us to check out what really counts with God by looking at a number of key episodes in the life of one of the most important figures in the Old Testament - King David of Israel. The study questions provided for each chapter make this an excellent resource for personal or group bible study

Also by Brian Johnston

Healthy Churches - God's Bible Blueprint For Growth

Hope for Humanity: God's Fix for a Broken World

First Corinthians: Nothing But Christ Crucified

Bible Answers to Listeners' Questions

Living in God's House: His Design in Action

Christianity 101: Seven Bible Basics

Nights of Old: Bible Stories of God at Work

Daniel Decoded: Deciphering Bible Prophecy

A Test of Commitment: 15 Challenges to Stimulate Your Devotion to Christ

John's Epistles - Certainty in the Face of Change

If Atheism Is True...

8 Amazing Privileges of God's People: A Bible Study of Romans 9:4-5

Learning from Bible Grandparents

Increasing Your Christian Footprint

Christ-centred Faith

Mindfulness That Jesus Endorses

Amazing Grace! Paul's Gospel Message to the Galatians

Abraham: Friend of God

The Future in Bible Prophecy

Unlocking Hebrews

Learning How To Pray - From the Lord's Prayer

About the Bush: The Five Excuses of Moses
Deepening Our Relationship With Christ
Really Good News For Today!
A Legacy of Kings - Israel's Chequered History
Minor Prophets: Major Issues!
The Tabernacle - God's House of Shadows
Tribes and Tribulations - Israel's Predicted Personalities
Once Saved, Always Saved - The Reality of Eternal Security
After God's Own Heart : The Life of David
Jesus: What Does the Bible Really Say?
God: His Glory, His Building, His Son
The Feasts of Jehovah in One Hour
Knowing God - Reflections on Psalm 23
Praying with Paul
Get Real ... Living Every Day as an Authentic Follower of
Christ
A Crisis of Identity
Double Vision: Hidden Meanings in the Prophecy of Isaiah
Samson: A Type of Christ

About the Author

Born and educated in Scotland, Brian worked as a government scientist until God called him into full-time Christian ministry on behalf of the Churches of God (www.churchesofgod.info). His voice has been heard on Search For Truth radio broadcasts for over 30 years (visit www.searchfortruth.podbean.com) during which time he has been an itinerant Bible teacher throughout the UK and Canada. His evangelical and missionary work outside the UK is primarily in Belgium and The Philippines. He is married to Rosemary, with a son and daughter.

About the Publisher

Hayes Press (www.hayespress.org) is a registered charity in the United Kingdom, whose primary mission is to disseminate the Word of God, mainly through literature. It is one of the largest distributors of gospel tracts and leaflets in the United Kingdom, with over 100 titles and hundreds of thousands despatched annually. In addition to paperbacks and eBooks, Hayes Press also publishes Plus Eagles Wings, a fun and educational Bible magazine for children, and Golden Bells, a popular daily Bible reading calendar in wall or desk formats. Also available are over 100 Bibles in many different versions, shapes and sizes, Bible text posters and much more!